REVERIES

IN SEARCH OF LOVE, HOPE, & COURAGE

First published in 2021 by the Light of Healing Hope Foundation

Copyright © 2021 Alexandra Villard de Borchgrave

Photographs and illustrations Copyright © Getty Images and © Dreamstime.

Creative Direction: Alexandra Villard de Borchgrave
Design: Henrique Siblesz, enlinea design

Printed and bound in the United States by Quality Graphics and Printing, Inc.

10 9 8 7 6 5 4 3 2 1

Library of Congress Cataloging-in-Publication Data

De Borchgrave, Alexandra Villard.
REVERIES: In Search of Love, Hope, & Courage
Alexandra Villard de Borchgrave;
— 1st ed.

ISBN: 978-0-9914418-9-1

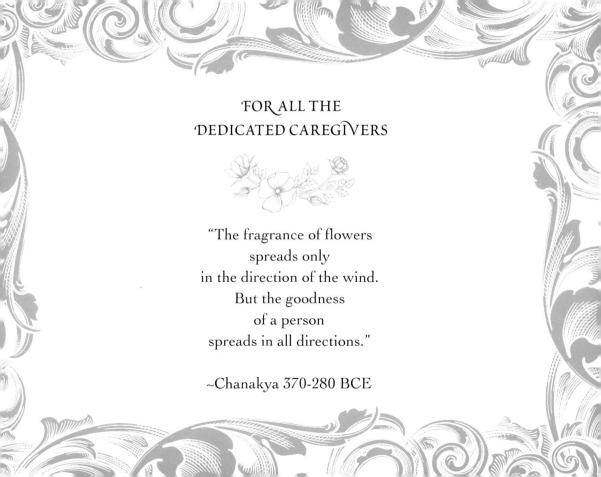

FOR ALL THE
DEDICATED CAREGIVERS

"The fragrance of flowers
spreads only
in the direction of the wind.
But the goodness
of a person
spreads in all directions."

~Chanakya 370-280 BCE

FOREWORD

Many of the best refreshing springs for love, faith, courage, and forgiveness can be found in Alexandra Villard de Borchgrave's books and journals provided by the Light of Healing Hope Foundation. During times of suffering, illness, conflict, strife, and fear they entice readers to step into beautiful images and poetic renderings with invitations to self-journaling.

As a chaplain, I've been privileged to present these precious materials as resources for discovery, recovery, and reconciliation to patients, families, staff, and hospice.

Guided by these resources one can stroll through nature, take on the strength of courageous lions, and soar with eagles through magnificent illustrations. In a journey through these treasures, resilience is birthed; courage finds its way to exhausted hearts; light loves its way through darkness; and strength finds the will to live.

What a delight it has been to witness a dementia patient connect with beautiful images of sunsets. What a joy it is to see pleasure spring on the face of a three year old distracted from stiches. One cannot estimate the therapeutic value realized for behavioral health patients who may believe their backs are against the wall. In addition, these books are like comforting hands gently touching the bereaved.

As we have moved with caution through the ups and downs of COVID-19 these treasures of the ordinary, presented in such extraordinary ways, have been instrumental in providing resiliency, faith, and hope to many.

With gratitude, joy, and love,

Rev. Dr. Alice V. Thompson,
Spiritual Care Coordinator
Calvert Health Medical Center

AWAKENINGS

ARISINGS

ASPIRATIONS

ALLEVIATIONS

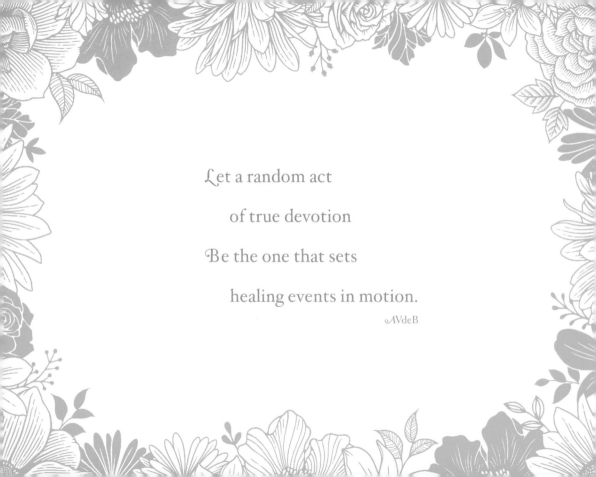

Let a random act

of true devotion

Be the one that sets

healing events in motion.

AVdeB

AWAKENINGS

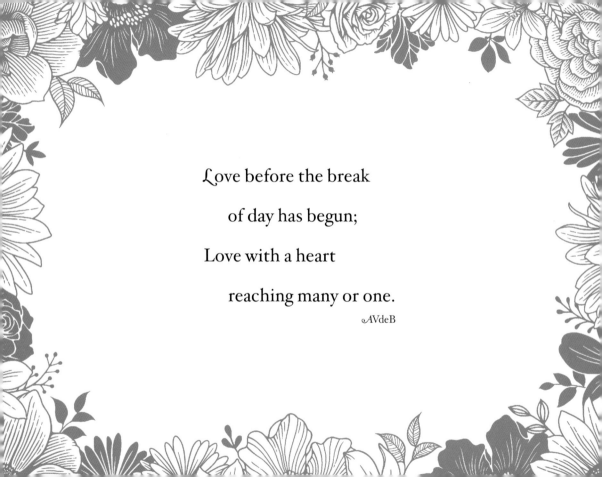

Love before the break

of day has begun;

Love with a heart

reaching many or one.

AVdeB

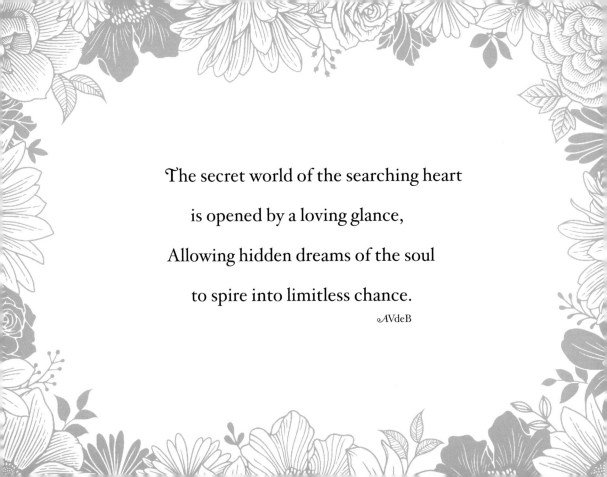

The secret world of the searching heart

is opened by a loving glance,

Allowing hidden dreams of the soul

to spire into limitless chance.

AVdeB

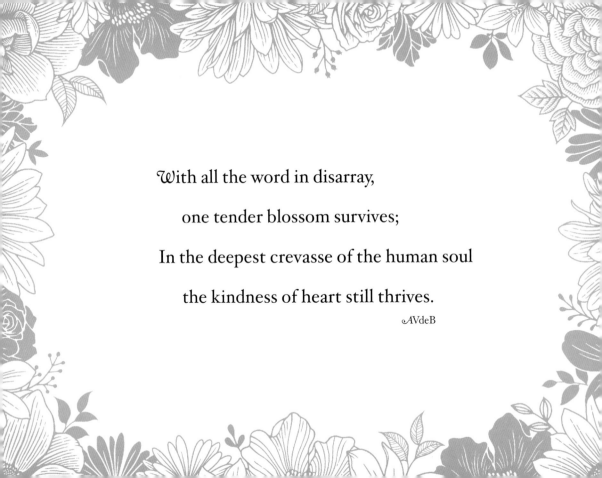

With all the word in disarray,

one tender blossom survives;

In the deepest crevasse of the human soul

the kindness of heart still thrives.

AVdeB

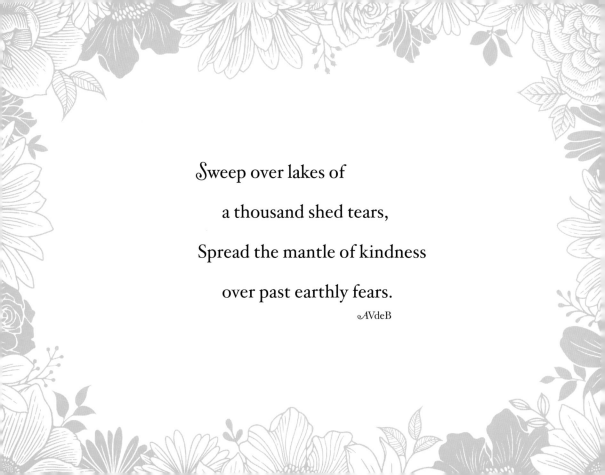

Sweep over lakes of

a thousand shed tears,

Spread the mantle of kindness

over past earthly fears.

AVdeB

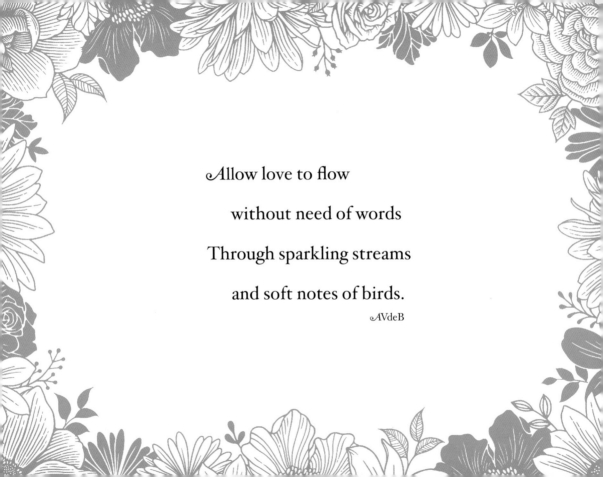

Allow love to flow

without need of words

Through sparkling streams

and soft notes of birds.

AVdeB

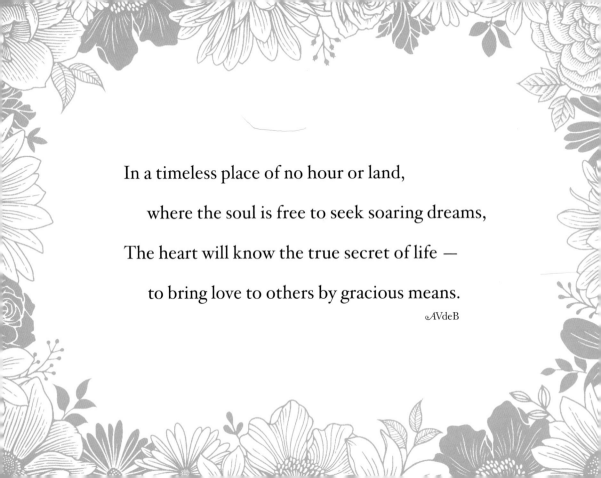

In a timeless place of no hour or land,

    where the soul is free to seek soaring dreams,

The heart will know the true secret of life —

    to bring love to others by gracious means.

AVdeB

Believe in the path

before your eyes,

Stay firm in virtue

and gracious devise.

AVdeB

ARISINGS

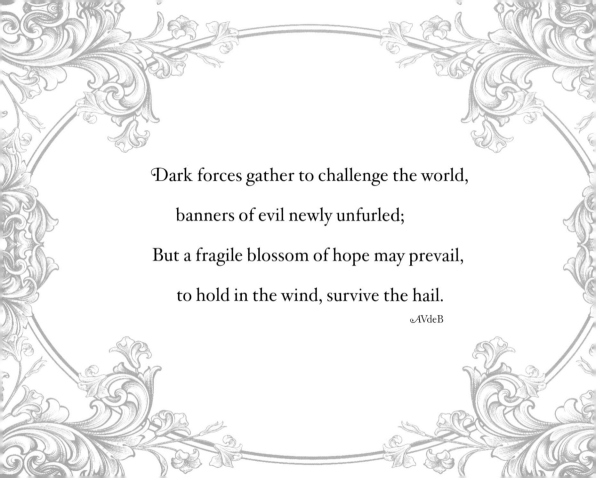

Dark forces gather to challenge the world,

banners of evil newly unfurled;

But a fragile blossom of hope may prevail,

to hold in the wind, survive the hail.

AVdeB

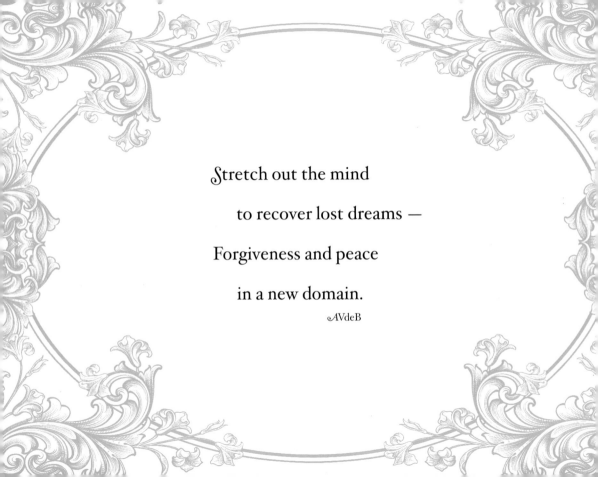

Stretch out the mind

to recover lost dreams —

Forgiveness and peace

in a new domain.

AVdeB

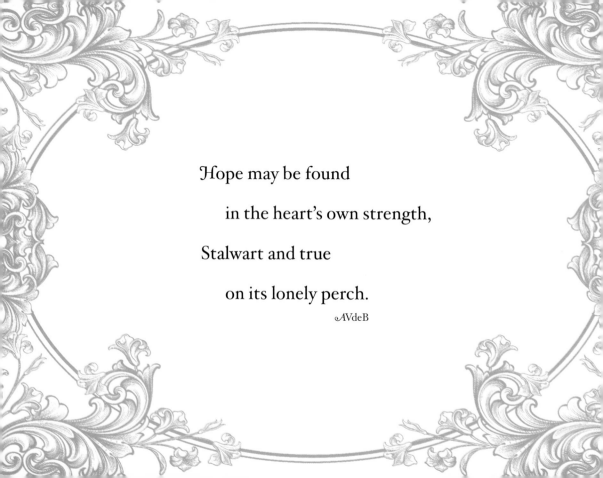

Hope may be found

    in the heart's own strength,

Stalwart and true

    on its lonely perch.

AVdeB

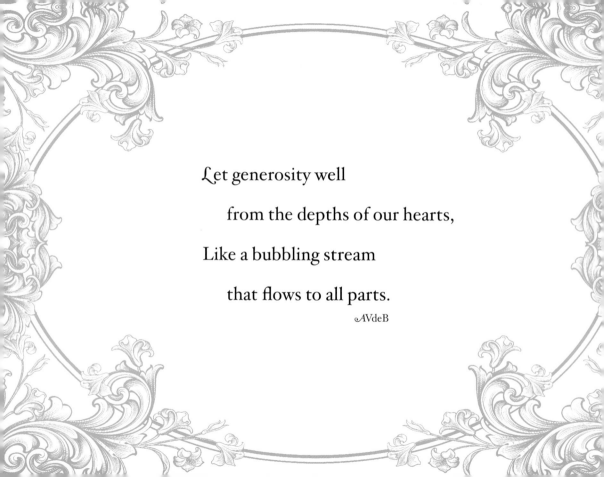

Let generosity well

from the depths of our hearts,

Like a bubbling stream

that flows to all parts.

AVdeB

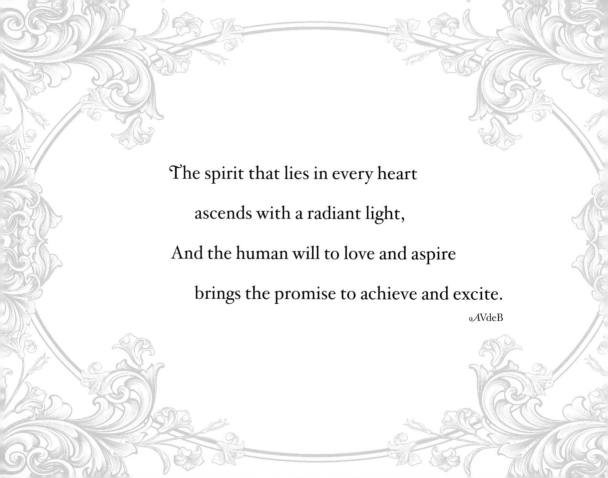

The spirit that lies in every heart

ascends with a radiant light,

And the human will to love and aspire

brings the promise to achieve and excite.

AVdeB

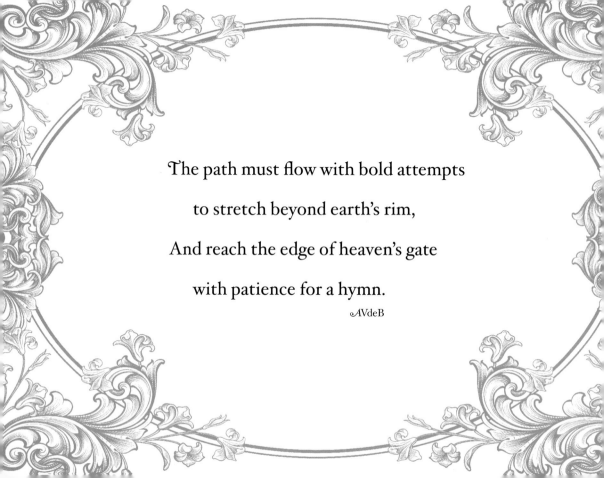

The path must flow with bold attempts

to stretch beyond earth's rim,

And reach the edge of heaven's gate

with patience for a hymn.

AVdeB

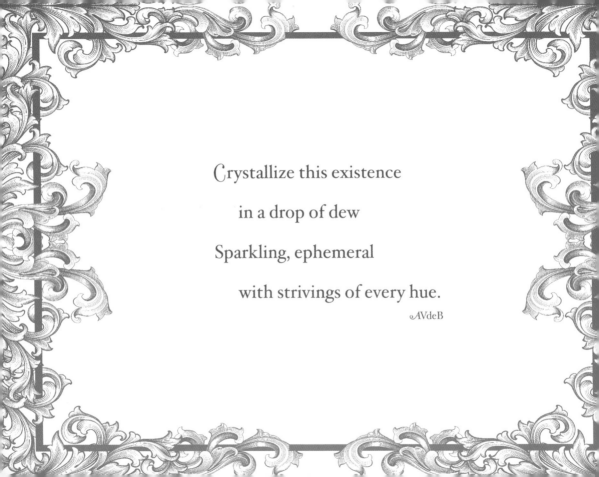

Crystallize this existence

in a drop of dew

Sparkling, ephemeral

with strivings of every hue.

AVdeB

ASPIRATIONS

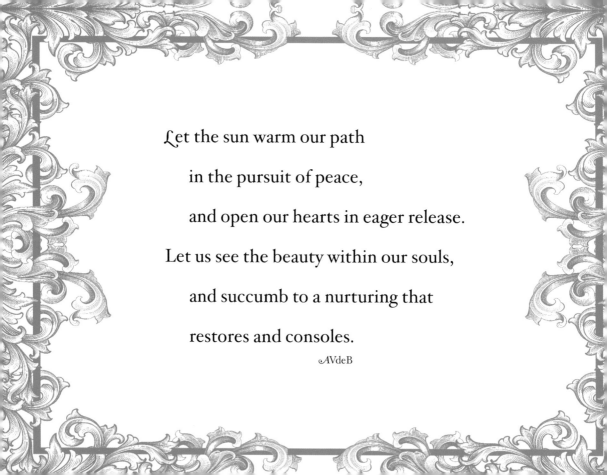

Let the sun warm our path

in the pursuit of peace,

and open our hearts in eager release.

Let us see the beauty within our souls,

and succumb to a nurturing that

restores and consoles.

AVdeB

Whatever the road

one takes in life,

Let it lead to

a wiser place.

AVdeB

May the fragrant scent of

the mimosa in white

Arouse our senses to

the world's healing light.

AVdeB

Resilience now may lead the soul

to grow with inner grace,

Drawing courage from its depth

to burst with ardent pace.

AVdeB

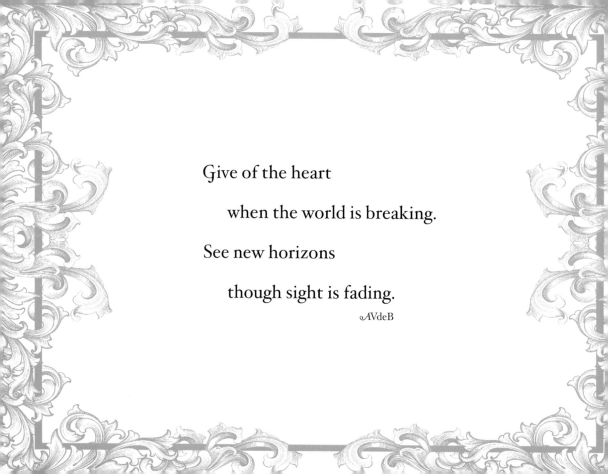

Give of the heart

  when the world is breaking.

See new horizons

  though sight is fading.

AVdeB

Savour the perfume

of exquisite days

While longing recedes

in the distant haze.

AVdeB

Treasure a love

that burns so fine

It defies the rule and

passage of time.

AVdeB

ALLEVIATIONS

Set the stars to be

    true companions this night;

And fill empty hearts

    with their lustrous light.

AVdeB

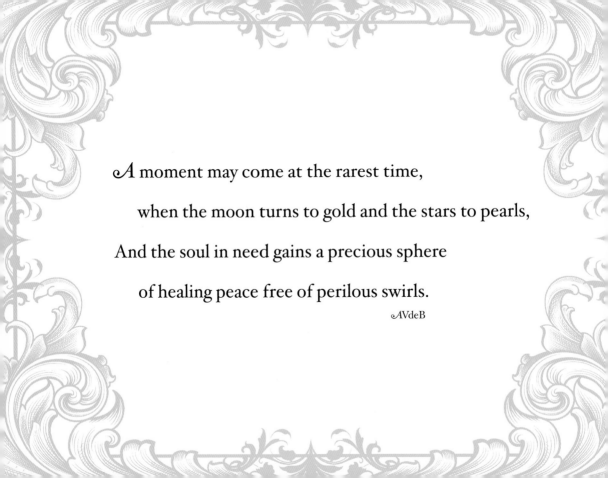

$\mathcal{A}$ moment may come at the rarest time,

when the moon turns to gold and the stars to pearls,

And the soul in need gains a precious sphere

of healing peace free of perilous swirls.

$\mathcal{A}$VdeB

Though the wounds of life may haunt the spirit,

unspeakable sorrow leaving ghosts of pain;

Abiding faith in the goodness of man,

allows love to transcend this earthly plain.

AVdeB

In an instant's bliss, when innocence thrives,

   and stars hang so low as to touch the heart,

The soul may arise to reach the divine,

   leaving imprints on earth as works of art.

AVdeB

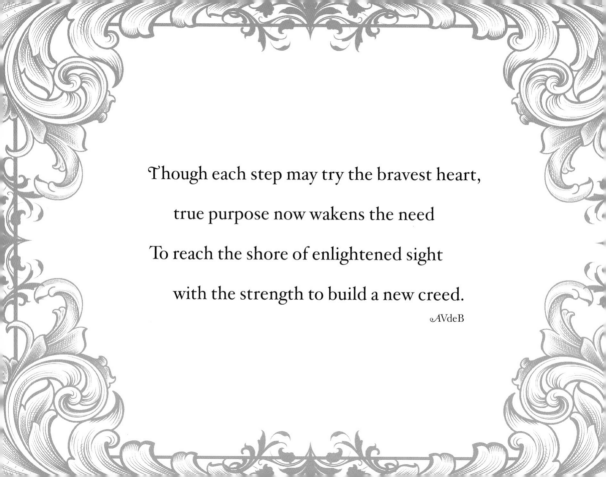

Though each step may try the bravest heart,

true purpose now wakens the need

To reach the shore of enlightened sight

with the strength to build a new creed.

AVdeB

May the night bring peace

at the end of the quest

When the mystery of life

is laid to rest.

AVdeB

ACKNOWLEDGMENTS

I cannot begin to thank all the immensely kind and generous supporters, including the wonderful members of the Light of Healing Hope Foundation's Board of Directors and Advisory Board, who have helped me on my journey to express messages of love, hope, and courage in the face of adversity.

I am deeply grateful to the countless compassionate souls who have made it possible for us to deliver over 60,000 books of hope to hospitals and hospices around the nation.

With their encouragement, I have connected verses I have written over many years with images of nature in this book as a new gift to continue our mission of comfort.

These years of creating books and journals would not have been possible without the exceptional design talent of Henrique Siblesz who has worked tirelessly by my side to bring as much beauty as possible to those in need, and I thank him with all my heart for his dedication.

In these challenging times, the extraordinary caregivers who give so much of themselves to help heal all of us, truly deserve to be honored. I have dedicated *Reveries* to these marvelous, selfless, and devoted people with my gratitude and love.

~ Alexandra Villard de Borchgrave

ARTWORK

COVER & ENDPAPERS

© borchee | Getty

BORDERS

© Getty

AWAKENINGS

1. © petrovaliliya | Getty

2. © Ondřej Prosický | Dreamstime

3. © Dorota Janus | Dreamstime

4. © BlackHoleSun Photography | Getty

5. © Nataba | Getty

6. © Volgariver | Dreamstime

ARISINGS

1. © Jurgita Juoniene | Dreamstime

2. © tak-photo | Getty

3. © Ondřej Prosický | Dreamstime

4. © Philip Steury | Dreamstime

5. © borchee | Getty

6. © Andrea Willmore | Dreamstime

ASPIRATIONS

1. © Sarayut Thaneerat | Dreamstime

2. © quickshooting | Getty

3. © miwa_in_oz | Getty

4. © pigphoto | Getty

5. © merc67 | Getty

6. © borchee | Getty

ALLEVIATIONS

1. © Trifonov_Evgeniy | Getty

2. © Marcus Gann | Dreamstime

3. © Biletskiy | Dreamstime

4. © den-belitsky | Getty

5. © eugenesergeev | Getty

6. © vvvita | Getty

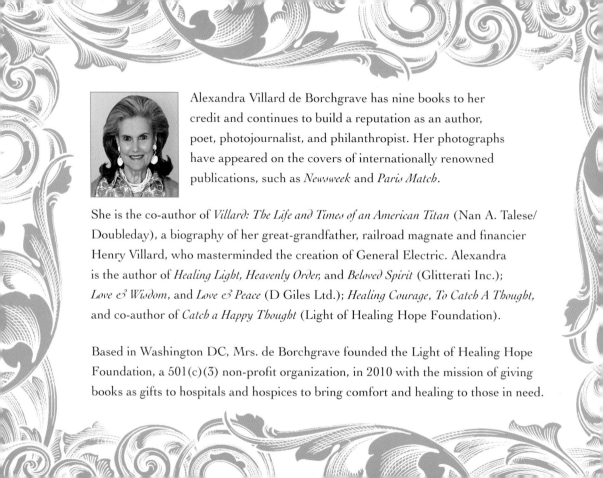

Alexandra Villard de Borchgrave has nine books to her credit and continues to build a reputation as an author, poet, photojournalist, and philanthropist. Her photographs have appeared on the covers of internationally renowned publications, such as *Newsweek* and *Paris Match*.

She is the co-author of *Villard: The Life and Times of an American Titan* (Nan A. Talese/ Doubleday), a biography of her great-grandfather, railroad magnate and financier Henry Villard, who masterminded the creation of General Electric. Alexandra is the author of *Healing Light, Heavenly Order,* and *Beloved Spirit* (Glitterati Inc.); *Love & Wisdom,* and *Love & Peace* (D Giles Ltd.); *Healing Courage, To Catch A Thought,* and co-author of *Catch a Happy Thought* (Light of Healing Hope Foundation).

Based in Washington DC, Mrs. de Borchgrave founded the Light of Healing Hope Foundation, a 501(c)(3) non-profit organization, in 2010 with the mission of giving books as gifts to hospitals and hospices to bring comfort and healing to those in need.